Beyond Existing

By Danielle Shorr

Beyond Existing
A collection of poems
By Danielle Shorr

This book is produced through the
Say Word Artist Development Program.
www.saywordla.org

Front cover coordinating by Sadie Goff with drawing by Julia Horwitz.

Interior illustrations by Julia Horwitz.

Editing, book layout, and back cover design by David A. Romero.
www.davidaromero.com

To contact the author, send an email to: daniellelshorr@gmail.com

TABLE OF CONTENTS

FOREWORD

I love how the mind can compile our most significant moments to remind us who we are. *Beyond Existing* is about me appreciating and learning from the most difficult obstacles, to the ugliest parts of myself, to the beautiful and miraculous healing of becoming stronger.

This book is where my hand, a crescent, has curled into a full moon with another. It is writing as liquid, all flowing, no pause, all heart. It is me and the one I love, smiling through cracked lips in a cold city, our warmth conquering the winter. It's in these moments, that I just start to grasp what it really means to be alive; that being here has to be more than a coincidence.

It is not always in the sweetness that I found revelation. Sometimes, it was the moments that were hardest to digest. When learning to cope, to recover, were more than an arm's reach away. It is my father's cancer, a fistfight with mental illness, the trauma I refused to name, and the lovers that left craters where their feet used to stand. I've learned that it takes more than just existing to get beyond these moments. Sometimes, refusing the stillness is the only option for survival we have. I understand now the consequences of silence. This is me choosing the only alternative I know, to be loud, to be unabashed, to celebrate, to be vulnerable, to understand that I am meant to be more than a quiet voice in a world that wears earplugs.

This book comes from the places where light doesn't shine, where my poetry became resilient and still grew in the dark. I am alive in the grit of teeth, in the soft space of the inner elbow, in the finger pads of my love. This book is about taking the time to reflect, to question, to allow yourself to listen, to speak, to breathe, to reward yourself for beating yesterday and diving face first into today.

No, this isn't my first day on this planet and it isn't yours either. But I wonder how would it be, if we lived, embracing it all? As if we were just now grasping what it means to be alive, beyond existing?

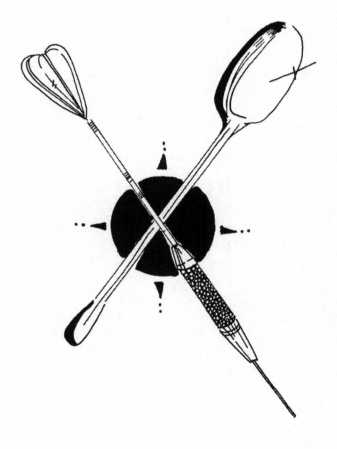

"Arrows" by Julia Horwitz

The hardest battle

The hardest battle of all is the one
you fight with yourself.
The hardest one to overcome is the one
nobody can see but you.
The worst enemy is the dull ache
dwelling underneath a bright smile.
One that has the capacity to make millions laugh.
One that succeeds in doing so
but happiness is not always gained
in knowing the number of lives impacted by yours.
Happiness is not defined by the amount of people who love you.
A crowded room is not a savior from drowning
and opens arms cannot always catch the falling.

There is no guide on how to wrestle your demons.
No clear solution on how to win.
Often times you will end up pinned to the ground.
Finding the strength to pull yourself up can be more than just a
challenge.
Depression is the cold war that nobody talks about.
The one they forget to mention in school.
We skip over it in textbooks and discussions,
assuming that if we forget its existence it will vanish completely,
but the only outcome of a closed mouth and stigma
is our own disappearance.
It will never be romantic to watch our loved ones fade
because they couldn't figure out how to love themselves enough
to stay.
It will never be desirable to turn to dust under bright lights
while the whole world watches in awe.

Depression,
is not something that can just be cured with chemicals
and someone to listen.
It is a constant struggle of living in an empty mansion

filled with hallways of locked doors
and spending every day of your life
trying to find a way out.
It is living in your body
but feeling like you're wearing someone else's skin.
It is watching excitement happen
but being unable to touch it, to taste it.
Tastes of kerosene and ethanol,
every missed step,
every small conflict is a lit match thrown into the pit of your
stomach.
Is unapologetic,
will take everyone you love and turn them into monster,
will take your reflection and turn it into ugly.

Depression,
will chew with sharp teeth
then spit you out to an unforgiving world
in crooked pieces.

There is no easy way to put yourself back together.
No telling of who is coming apart at the seams,
but the battle does not have to end
bloody,
in regret,
in what should have been done,
in what could have been prevented.
This battle is not going to cease
without a fair fight.
Do not give in,
even when your bones are purple and bruised,
your skin, ripped from sharpness.
Do not yield to disaster.
Do not succumb to darkness.
Do not surrender.
There is someone who will miss you.
Do not forfeit,

this battle is not through
and your story is not over
yet.

The moving on
is a crossword puzzle
I do not know the last answer to
there are fifteen spaces left
that I don't know how to fill
with anything other than you
there is so much empty
left over

It is much easier to hold on
to memories
and remnants
of what could have been
than it is to accept
a definite ending

Our future
may be dead
but you are still
very much alive in me

If I really tried
I bet I could forget you
but I don't think I want to
no, I don't think I do.

"Plant" by Julia Horwitz

Loving the addict

Loving the addict is
an addiction in itself.
Learning to digest
all of the sharp pieces that
come with it.
All of the apologies and how
they lose meaning
the second after they are said.
Loving the addict is
as much of an art as
the hiding,
the covering up,
as the forgive me.

After some time
I love you and I'm sorry
start to sound the same.
Letting go and withdrawal
become an equal amount
of swollen.
Coming back is
more relapse than any
tangible substance.

Loving the addict is
a guilty habit
growing inside a dark closet
feeding the plant until
it becomes animal,
ravenous.
Love and dependence
are diseases that
share the same root.

Being the addict
is always an attempted break up.
It is avoidance at
its finest.
It is ripping apart
threads of a rope
with chipped fingernails
in attempts to cut loose ends.
It is sawing pieces of
wood with bare skin
and trying not to get a splinter.
It is leave me.
It is don't go.
It is I am trying to not destroy
everything in my path.
It is painting with
heavy winds and rain,
hoping there wont be a mess to clean up.
Mess is as inevitable
as art is to creating.

Love and addiction
mix like oil and water.
Nobody is perfectly capable
of cleaning up correctly.
So we leave ourselves in a pile
to return to later.

Coming back is
more relapse than any
tangible substance
that has ever existed,
and mercy is more perilous
than we'd hope it to be.

How is it
that you can be loved
by so many
and still not love
yourself?

"The Liner" by Julia Horwitz

Amy
For Amy Winehouse

Amy is a crooning bird
with beehive nest built from soul.
She is sixty five years drowned inside the body of a young girl.
Loves jazz and destructive boys.
Looks at him the way her voice does microphone.
Eyes are drawn black like a cat's,
she sings the way its tail curls along wood floor
graceful,
effortless,
confident.

Shaina Maidel,
with a gap between her two front bent teeth,
echoed laugh and studded diamond above her lip.
Jewish girl,
who wears Star of David around her neck belts.
Songs she writes with scratching fingers
against ink covered arms.
Pretty girl loves heroin
and crack pipe
and liquor.
She has a crooked mouth but hums melodies
smooth as the heart is aching.

Pink ballet slippers stained red
from pricks between toes.
Bulimia makes a home in her habits.
Empties her stomach after every meal.
Makes more room for wine and vodka and whiskey with Coke.
Stumbles across a stage she does not belong to
while the audience boos and mocks,
while the paparazzi stalks and preys,
while the media criticizes
and a world that doesn't quite understand does the same.

We watch her like a disaster
a car accident,
unable to stop staring at the damage.
We watch her downfall like
an avalanche in a city not our own
so we do nothing to save it.

This disappearing act is not magic
but a side effect of fame unwanted.
Dad doesn't understand that skin and bones
is the foreshadowing of death.
Says, "Baby, smile for the camera."
"Baby, just do what you're supposed to."
"Baby, just finish the tour."
Sucks every last ounce out of her
like the wringing of a towel.
It is an easy thing for a girl to become invisible
when she wants to bad enough.

A crooning bird falls from a tree.
We watch with hands at our side,
bodies tilted in confusion.
What a shame, we say.
There is depth but it is hiding under addiction.
All we see is girl destroying herself
under the fluorescent lights we placed above her head.
What a waste, we say,
shaking heads.
We do nothing in response.

My love,
you tore boundaries with your swollen hands.
They said your honest was too loud,
hair too big,
voice too bold.
They picked at you with curious fingers.
Gap-toothed Jew girl

with the audacity to break the silence,
ended up breaking too.

Shaina Maidel,
with a space between her two front bent teeth.
Echoed laugh and studded diamond above her lip.
Jewish girl who they never thought could be a star
became just that.
Burned into supernova
graceful
effortless
confident
in her descent
back to
black.

Chicago
- After Carl Sandburg

The neighbor's dogs howl in response to police sirens
and so does my Midwestern heart.
It is 60 degrees in early November
here in Southern California.
Some think that's enough
to call cold.

I laugh at the acknowledgments
of the change in weather
and the proclamations of chill in the air,
proud in the certainty
that this,
is truly the closest we'll ever get to the arctic.

But, the cold is not a few days without sun
or
an inch or two of rain
or
the change that comes with daylight savings
and a 5 o'clock sunset.

Cold
is seeing your breath under streetlights.
It is holding it on the walk home from dinner.
It is grabbing for a hand through a glove too thin
and pulling fabric over purple lips.
It is watching snow build a shell outside your front door
to keep you from escaping.
It is admiring the coating of landscape through a window,
without ever complaining about the temperature.

Cold,
is the ringing of one too many bullets skipping

and the sirens crawling behind,
always a few seconds too late.

After a man bends down in front you
pretending to drop something
in order to violate you on his way up

We giggle,
like young girls at the mall
being followed by boys
who don't know
how to take
refusal with grace.

Young girls,
on a walk home from school
and a car following behind,
a little too close.

Young girls,
who breathe relief at every story
their mother says
could have easily been them.

Young girls,
who go to the bathroom
in groups for a reason.

Young girls,
who fake phone calls at the bus stop
with exceptional talent.

We chuckle,
making a defense mechanism
out of discomfort
for the first time.

It's always in retrospect,
the fighting back.
It's always fist and rage

and all the opposite of what a lady is supposed to be.
The politeness drained from flesh into blue fingertips
ready to carve the man out from his body.
All nails and weighted hands.
Looking back at the moment
the girl in us
tells the woman in us
we are to laugh it off,
toss back in humor and walk blindly forward.
Hold this head high
with years of loose threads.
Keep it from tilting,
trading anger for ignorance.
Replacing reaction with a lack of.
Swallowing pride,
because it has always been
safer than resistance.

It's the minutes after
when I imagine what I didn't do.
A stranger,
crouches consciously to invade space
he knows damn well isn't his.
I watch the image of his smiling satisfaction
as he continues on.
I try to make excuses,
maybe it's a mistake
but if it's a mistake
it wouldn't be given away
by the corners of his lips stretching outward,
meticulous.

I picture my knee charging into his teeth,
the impact of muscle against face.
I wonder if he'd still be grinning
with the blood staining his mouth.
I think about my tongue doing more than sitting still.

Say my body's not the only weapon I have to show.
Scream so loud that the whole bar turns ahead to pay attention.
Remember the pepper spray hanging from my purse.
Remember that its existence is only ever remembered
after the fact.

And my laugh,
never enough voice
to knock the guts
it took for him to touch me
back into his stomach.
My bravery,
never enough courage to
take the fear out of risk.

I am,
a response without a throat
and my silence,
the regret that wins most often.

We giggle,
because it's what we know best.
Like we are well aware of the fact
that we didn't have all these years of practice
for nothing.

For the girl who doesn't know how to say "no"

I have been a version of you too many times.
I have worn your body on frequent occasions.
Always neutral, stock-still,
denying purpose into static,
eyes open
and breathing.
I know exactly
how to refuse
or resist when rough palms press on my skin.
I know what it is
to feel like there is no other option,
but to lie still
while eager hands pull at your body,
uninvited lips stepping into your mouth.
How quickly a tongue can become a weapon?
I know it all too well,
the iron-clenched fists,
the unforgiving friction,
and how disintegration becomes second nature.

For a girl whose limbs
are already paper-made,
stares burn into too many white walls.
A woman watching her own shadow
and the word "no" never escapes the vocal chords.
There is never a question to answer to.
It is assumed,
that our shared pulse is enough "yes."
Consent is an easy thing to ignore
when it is hardly ever asked for.
Men are taught to halt,
only if it is preceded by screeching.
I wonder how many silent cries
are covered by darkness and heavy breathing.

This is for the girl
who doesn't know how to say "NO."
For the girl who has played mime too many times.
For the girl who has been made surface to sandpaper hands.
For the girl who is always vocal,
but in a single instant became victim to chokehold silence.
This is for you.

I have been a version of you too many times.
I have worn the fingerprints on your phosphorescent skin.
I have pulled off your clothing after a night of detachment.
I see you in every mirror I look into,
every stained glass reflection.
I hear you every time he doesn't ask.
It is so easy to forget you have a voice,
but I know with certainty that you do.
I know that you understand the stillness,
the quiet,
the hush,
the absence of language.
Your words held hostage.
You are the only one
who bares the heaviness of night kneeling on your chest,
the added weight from all those
who have touched you without permission.

I want you to know,
I would carry it for you if I could.
I want you to know
it is not your fault
that your calmness
is often mistaken for compliance.
It is not your fault
that you so quickly fall paralyzed.
Playing statue may seem
like the easy way out
but you were never meant

to stand still.
You were made
to howl our names into the ground,
until the forest shakes its trees to their death,
and no one is around
to hear it.
You were made to bellow your refusal into the night
until it wakes every sleeping soul
who has forgotten your existence.
You were made to be woman.
You were made to be loud.
You are meant to be heard.
Do not let the silencer of his body, turned gun,
convince you of anything else.
I can hear you,
they can too.

Socialized advice to women

Smile more,
but keep your happiness elusive.
Only show it to the world when prompted.
Wear your heart on your sleeve.
Make sure it doesn't bleed openly.
Don't be too sensitive or weak.
Don't find disgust in violence.
Don't cringe at gore.
Don't talk about your period.
Don't talk about yourself.
Don't talk.

You're perfect as is
but try this tea
juice
cleanse
who needs food anyway
detox
waist trainer
modern day corset
diet
diet
diet.
Suffocate your organs into a
cast until they forget why they exist.
Your body can't remember why
it ever wanted to be anything but content.

Be confident,
comfortable.
Get your bikini body
get summer ready.
Grow your ass,
shrink everything else.
How dare you find pride in your skin,

in the excess of it.
How dare you face the sun
without attempting to cower in its presence.

Be modest
like you weren't born naked.
Be mother
like you are only good for your uterus.
Be more than your womanhood.
Don't be a feminist
Be one of the men
but don't demand equality.
Ask politely
and you still won't get it.

Hold your own opinions,
not too tightly.
Strong beliefs make you crazy.
Any belief makes you crazy.
Crazy if you disagree.
Crazy if you fight back.
Don't be a pushover.

Laugh out.
Grow in.
Expand.
Keep to yourself.
Speak up.
Don't say too much.

Smile
Smile
Smile,
Don't let the world see your teeth bent.
Be anything but
crooked,
smile.

Believe and you can be anything
that isn't what you are already.

"Broken Mirror" by Julia Horwitz

It's the broken pieces that make us who we are.
It's the same ones that others find the most beauty in.

My brother breaks my chin when I am four.
A man I'm with now
who I don't yet love
tells me that it is his favorite part about me.
He can't explain why but he likes the part of my face
that is crooked.

The doctor sews me back together with stitches,
twice the amount of my age.
The man I am with now is older,
but he says he is just young enough for it to be okay.

My brother's guilt is written on his face,
I forgive him for a candy bar.
When I am angry, the man I'm with now, offers me apology
in the form of affection.

10 year old me has a centimeter scar that goes unnoticed,
only making an appearance when my head is held high enough.
When we argue
I become the Taurus that the stars have written me to be.
I don't give in without a fight.

My brother's apologies
have always been in the form of chocolate
and my mercy has always been to eat it.
I still grant forgiveness without it being warranted.

My father says to forgive him.
Oh, the things we are willing to forget in exchange for ease.
I'll say I'm sorry to avoid stretching the tension further,
do anything to break the space between us.

The moment the bandage left my face,
the memory left my brother's mind.
Even with the reminder still living on my skin.
Lover and I never talk past the surface,
for fear of sinking too deeply into one another.

I run a fingertip along the rough of my edges,
more proud than bitter.

This is just another way that I've become who I am.
A man I was with didn't love me
and didn't know if he ever would.

I leave before I find out.

Last texts (in alphabetical order)

Are you mad at me?
Babe
Baby
Don't please
Goodnight
Goodbye
I was
I'll call you tonight
I'm in front of your door
I'm sorry
It happens
It was sad seeing it get colder
K.
Ok sweetheart, sleep well
OK
Okay
Okay fine
We'll talk soon
What about you?
Where have you been
Where did you go?
Sorry
Sorry.
Sorry
Sorry, I really am
Sorry
You still up?

Scale

You are too familiar with yourself,
with your face,
your body,
your beauty.

Your reflection is an image skewed
from being seen by your same eyes too often.
Your confidence is a locked box
you keep in the back of your closet.
Your smile is more uncomfortable
than it is curling.
You've grown to hate the large of your laugh.

You are blind to almost all that you are.

Just imagine,
for a second
what you look like
to someone who is a stranger.
You could be their textbook definition of ideal.
Their exact description of beautiful
and you wouldn't even know it.

Imagine for a moment,
how your greatness might resonate,
with someone who has never been close to that much at once.

There have been people in your life
who have attempted to break you into smaller pieces,
crush you whole so you would be easier to swallow.

There will always be someone who will be unable
to see your worth.
Others, who won't be able to handle you.
Maybe they'll see too much and try to shrink you into less

with the hopes of becoming more themselves.
You build yourself quieter each time that you do.
You know how to shy away from the presence of light.
You've settled comfortably in the corners,
but there is someone out there waiting to hear your loud.
A blank canvas ready to be filled with all of your paint.
You will be the exact shade they have spent their entire life
trying to find.

When they do,
you'll remember that there was a time
before you were taught to see dark
when you could see every hue
without squinting.

"Moon" by Julia Horwitz

Snapple fact

I once read
that in 7.6 billion years
the sun
having reached its maximum size
will shine 3,000 times brighter
than it does now.
I have always wondered
how it is possible
to know such a thing.
When 100 years
is beyond a lifetime,
how we could possibly
look so far into the future
when now seems like an eternity
and tomorrow is miles away.
How can we embrace the moment
when we are constantly being told to plan ahead?
What's the point
of waiting 7.6 billion years
when the sun is already
shining
and the moon
already loves her?

21 ways to believe in God:

1. Spend a night in your arms.

2. Stand in a room full of people who love you.

3. Stand in a room full of strangers who love the same things
   but hardly know each other,
   dancing in unison to a song they have all found a savior in.

4. A Los Angeles sunset.

5. An Idaho sunrise.

6. Loving a person who reciprocates.

7. Laying next to someone you love,
   with their face lit by a glow from the television.

8. The firework of your laughter.

9. A Sunday morning, our legs intertwined,
   the crack of light peeking
   through a window to wake us.

10. When you are certain what you want your future to look like.

11. To be able to relive magic again and again.

12. Every second that passes with us together.
    Every one that drags when we're separate.

13. Have you ever had a hummingbird teach you what grace is?

14. Have you ever seen a sunflower with a center as wide as your
    fist?

15. Every person you've met with a heart bigger than that
    sunflower.

16. If you've ever asked yourself why am I here?

17. Being okay not knowing the answer.

18. I am running out of ways to say
      that love is synonymous with a name
      I've never felt comfortable pronouncing.

19. I believe it more every time I catch you looking at me.

20. The reasons are infinite.

21. After some time,
      I stopped counting.

Love,
when right
will make every day
feel like a Sunday morning.

Proclamation

I find comfort in the static of the record player humming,
the crackling of vinyl against its holding.
Your arms tucked tight around the curve of my spine
and waking up to the corners of your lips widening.

This is a Sunday morning
that I could relive
seven days a week.

This is a feeling
I am near terrified of
but in the best way possible.

I have never been one for writing love poems,
when it comes to writing love,
because happy endings aren't my specialty.

I'm not one for spilling vulnerability
to then have to clean up the mess.

I'm not the best at predicting the future
and letting go
is an art form
I am still mastering.

I have never been one for writing love poems
especially not for those
who don't stick around
long enough to hear them
but for you
I am willing to take the risk,
to set aside hesitation
for the chance of lasting,
to sacrifice my fear of heights
for the possibility of a smooth landing.

I don't know you well
but I know you enough
to know you're exactly what I want.

So I'll talk about your smile.
How your dimples have quickly become
my favorite half-moon to stare at,
or the way you look at me
like a single star
in the middle of a busy Los Angeles sky.

Being enfolded in your grasp
feels like the sun peeking through the gray.
How light makes itself known
even in the midst of rain.

I want my skin
to find a home in your palms
and my laugh,
an echo in the crook of your neck.

For routine to settle
on the map of your body
from collarbone to knuckle to wrist,
making a transparent dent in each earlobe
missing the touch my lips
to crave the caress of my hands
when they have other obligations.

I'll hope
that I can waste
as much time with you
as I intend to.
Although I'm sure
that any time we spend together
would be anything but wasted.

I hope that we can stretch these two nights
into two hundred.
Weaving a weekend into something we can wrap ourselves in.

This is me saying a prayer
the only way I know how to.

I have never been one for writing love poems
but for you
it is all I want to do.
Listen to the silence
and from it
form a symphony.
Take this coincidence
and call it fate.
To give out all of my honesty
and hope that you stay.

Appetite

I have never felt more okay
to eat two cinnamon rolls in one sitting,
or go for ice cream even after we've had dinner.
Maybe it's your hand on my stomach
tracing the soft as it rolls over.
Maybe it's the way you think I deserve
to eat all of the chocolate in the world
or how you always share your fries with me
when I feel too guilty to get my own.
Maybe it's how I'm no longer scared of being content,
How I'd rather count your eyelashes individually
than every calorie I've consumed this week.
I learned how to obsess
about something other than my eating habits
I've found relief in your staying.

We are a taste
incapable of becoming too saccharine.
My appetite for us grows
as days fall beneath us.
I'm certain I will never
know hunger to be
a desperate cause.

This is our love.
My stomach full
and my heart,
equally filled.

Love letter to my thighs

Dear thickness,
Dear bold flesh I call a shelter.
My protection for this body I call home.

Dear thighs,
you are more important than you think.
More crucial than you've been told.
More space than I know what to do with
and more vocal than other girls' quiet
but your prominence is nothing to hide.
Your existence is not an apology ready to be given.
Your presence does not want to be covered.
The way you suffocate yourself into a pair of jeans
is a talent unlike any other.
On hot summer days when skin comes out
to kiss itself between your graces
what some would call chub rub,
I call magic.

Thighs,
you never let clothing,
or temperature,
or weather come between you.
You are a passionate lover,
the proud I always strive to be,
the unapologetic beauty
I wish was all of me.
You maintain the confidence I have to dig for
in every other part of my body.
You have so much potential built into layers of thick.
You've been told you save lives.

There have been times when I neglected you.
I have been blind in acknowledging your worth.
It is not an easy feat,

to love the parts of yourself
we are taught from
an early age to hate.
Magazines have always said be small
while you have always aimed to be big.
Trends telling you to downsize
when all you've ever wanted is to grow,
expand into a galaxy built of freckles and skin.
You are as human as human as gets.

I am sorry I have made you into a war zone.
I am sorry that this world has twisted your greatness
into embarrassment.
I am sorry that people have tried to make an apology
out of your density.
I am sorry that we live in a society that keeps telling you
to shrink.
I am sorry I have wanted you to.

It has taken me years to be thankful for your holy.
You are the answer to my every prayer.
You are living proof of survival.

Thighs,
this is my proclamation of appreciation.
This is my asking forgiveness.
I never meant to make you feel anything but needed.

Thighs,
you were not made to be thin,
you were not meant to be shy,
you were built to be the loudest voice in every room.
Head turning, eye catching, without remorse,
you are never silent,
even when I am.
For that,
I love you.

Strength

Strength,
is not a flattened stomach with
a mountain range of abs,
nor is it a back
with symmetrical indents.
It is not how much you can lift
or how much you can carry
but rather,
how you carry it.

Sometimes strength is only going to one class
but still going.
Sometimes it is only getting one thing done on today's list
but still getting something done.
Sometimes strength is a bare face willing to leave the house.
Sometimes it is just getting yourself to leave the house at all.

Strength looks like feeding yourself
even though you're not starving.
It is teeth brushing,
hair washing,
even if it's only once a week.
Laundry, now and then.
Enough water to keep hydrated.
It is two socks, probably unmatched,
a shirt, pants, and maybe a bra.
The breath it takes to put them on,
to walk outside,
to be human.

Sometimes strength is a bit of last night's dinner
stuck to the side of a plate
still holding on
or the spider from underneath the couch
attempting to survive another day,

uncertain
but determined.

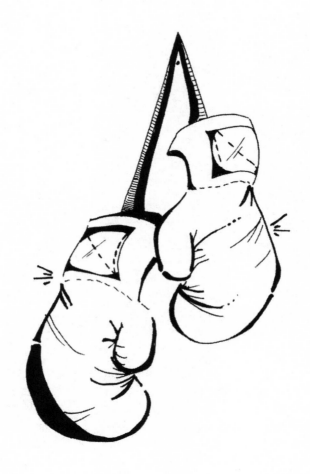

"Boxing Gloves" by Julia Horwitz

Survival

I lose count of how many times I am catcalled
on my way to the gym
I think that maybe turning around,
eating an entire pizza and never coming back,
would stop this from happening
I realize it wouldn't,
I would still be a woman.

"Smile baby,"
I hear as I leave my car.
Just 3 hours of sleep to get me to where I am.
I am tired enough to silence a response from my middle finger
but not enough to quit.

A guy standing at the bus stop sees my hands wrapped
Tells me that boxing is sexy.
I wonder how clenched fists,
self-protection
and the desire to make it home alive each night
is sexy?

When I don't hit the bag hard enough
I remember the force of his body.
I let my knuckles do the speaking.
There is no stopping after the rage is reborn.

A man tells me how lucky I am
to have this figure.
Ignorant to the fact that hard work
is nothing remotely similar to luck.
My body has become a string
I have been stretching and pulling to make stronger.
Luck,
is something he'll never have enough of to touch me again.

I like the way it feels
to be sore from something willingly.
To get up from the ground
without a hand helping.
These bruises are proof of my living.

I have been practicing my run,
to make up for all of the times
I haven't had the guts to
My intuition is reaching out for
every time I've held it back.

I like to say that survival
is a choice made in the aftermath of destruction.
The conscious decision to chew through broken glass
rather than swallow it whole
Survival is not as simple as I didn't die
it is refusing not to.

Hand squeezing wrist,
he told me I'd never be enough for anyone.
Today,
I am enough for me.

I'm working on myself
for myself
building ash into muscle.
This is strength learning
how to pull through.
This is me doing exactly that.

Nature doesn't let
cement stop it
from growing.
It manages
to peek out
through sidewalks
and concrete.
Nature doesn't let
anything stop it
from existing.

So tell me,
what's your excuse?

Let Him

Let him miss you.
Let him roll over in the morning to find you gone,
your absence filling the empty side of the bed like a flood.
He will drown before he even wakes up.
Let him know what it's like to have the sheets to himself
when his hands reach out to find too much space to grab,
a vacant imprint of you still on the mattress.
Let him crave the hold of your body against his,
laying down, molded together in unison.
Let him miss the crook of your neck
and how his face fit perfectly in it
like a hollowed shell.
Let him miss your skin and his own announcement of its softness.
Let him miss how your fingers would run swiftly along
the folds and creases.
Let him miss the tracing of your veins that led him home,
a blue reminder of familiarity.
Let him miss your legs folding between his while sleeping.
Let him miss your breath in his ear.
Let him miss your words blanketing around his fears,
how your language was the only kind capable
of calming his stress.

Let him miss your comfort like a Midwest winter
without a fireplace to lay in front of,
like below zero temperatures with a broken furnace.
Let him feel his heart leave his chest
when he thinks he sees you at the store,
at a concert, bar,
a restaurant,
all of the places he knows you aren't.
He will look for you anyway.

Let his lips mumble your memory
with every shot of whiskey that meets his mouth.

Let him taste you with each cigarette he smokes
with the intention of forgetting.
Let him hear your voicemail when he calls you at 3 am.
Let him leave his drunken words
in a mailbox you will never check.
Let him say your name in his sleep.
Let him wonder where you are tonight.
Let him feel your ache in every muscle,
every bone, every limb.
Let him wonder if you're aching too.
Don't give him the satisfaction of knowing you are.

Don't tell him you are splitting like the red sea,
your heart spilling.
Don't let him know you are near freezing to death
without palms to protect you from the cold.
How this December was one for the records.
You will look back and wonder how you ever managed to
survive.

Don't let him know that getting up and out of bed
is a ropes course.
Don't let him know that every bit of ink
made permanent on your body
is too much reminder to look at,
The words are growing into unwanted by the second.
Don't let him know that tonight you are too far from the sun
to expand.
You are shrinking from the darkness
and you don't know how to let the light back in.
Don't let him believe that your smile is anything but
a portfolio of happiness.
Don't let him know that your laugh
is merely a symphony crafted from regret.
Don't let him know that he is the ringing in your ear
refusing to go away.
Don't let him know you still crave him like a bad addiction,

the withdrawal being the worst it's ever been.
Do not let him know you miss him.
There is no purpose in missing what never made you whole.
You are enough human without someone to need you.
If he misses you tonight, let him
If you miss him tonight,
don't.

Corrosion

You know how coffee starts to smell
like cigarettes after it sits for a while?
You know when you stare at a word
for too long,
it starts to look uncomfortable?
You know how anything can change
if it goes without being touched?
Isn't it funny how things morph
right before our eyes?
Isn't it strange how the shift happens,
slowly,
but visible?
Is this what will become of us?
Will I be a bitter taste in your mouth
if I overstay my welcome?
The coat of dust
on an object forgotten?
Something sweet
that broke down too sour?
The sand that lingers
from a past trip to the beach?
A granulated reminder of better times?
How do I keep from turning into a liquid
you pour down your sink?
How do I hold color without rusting?
How do I stand still without growing dull?
How do I remain what you love most?
How do I remain a thing you love at all?

You weren't as great
as I painted you out to be.
Maybe I'm just a good artist.

Google search

Today, I did not think about him.
It is the first time in an entire year that I haven't.
I didn't realize this until the day was almost gone.

Today I went to lunch,
did laundry,
drove to the gym.
I didn't see his shadow in my rearview mirror.
It is the first time during a commute
I don't feel the overwhelming urge to pull over.
The speed of the traffic mixed
with the acceleration of my thoughts
guides me to the side of the road,
anxiety blowing loudly through the vents into my open mouth
until I am too tired to focus.
Today is the first time that didn't happen.

Last week I googled "therapists near me."
I settled on a woman with a nice smile and a specialty for trauma.
This is the first time I find myself familiar with that word.
It was almost comfortable like a distant family member
I am just now recognizing.
Trauma is something with one definition
but many faces.
For the past eight months I have been wearing his.

On Monday I spend an hour in the office of a stranger.
She asks me why I'm here.
I respond with "I don't know."
My answer is as dishonest as my avoidance of her question.
She asks me how I am.
I almost forget that I didn't come all this way to say "fine."
For a moment I almost forget that I am not.

I tell her how sometimes laying in bed
becomes catalyst to chest pain.
Some nights I can still feel him kneeling on top of my chest,
Pressing his body into cracked ribs,
feel the spit on my neck,
his humming of a song they play too often on the radio.
There is no trigger warning
for the reminders life has to offer.
I find them everywhere without trying

Today I did not think about him.
Yesterday I did not think about him.
The day before, I only thought about myself.
There is very real possibility
that my mind could figure out a way
to bring back the unwanted.
Tomorrow could be another way to remember,
but today I didn't.

I went to lunch,
did laundry,
drove to the gym.
I made it home without incident
not perfect,
but it is an accomplishment
nonetheless.

**When the elevator won't close
and you are standing
awkwardly in it avoiding eye contact with me**

You say,
"This is awkward,"
the way most people point out that it's raining.
Your hand is on the button,
your eyes are on the ground
and I'm waiting to go up while
you're waiting to go down.
It's funny you find this so awkward.
Maybe it's because you wear coward so well
and I, lioness.
I greet you well with grinning teeth
and confidence.
In this very moment, technology
and its failure
have become my new favorite
elephant in the room,
stomping about blindly,
pushing its trunk into the space between us.
I love this discomfort.
I love the tension thick as rope.
I love that you probably wish you could tie it around your neck
right now.
I stare directly into you,
because I love feeding the caged animal.
I am an intentional catalyst
for your internal, "Oh fuck."
Is this what happens
when there is too much weakness
on one side for closure?
When the scales shift to the right
and the left falls off completely?
Does it make you uneasy
that I still exist after you stopped talking to me?

Bless this elevator's malfunctioning,
how grateful I am for the comedy,
for these few minutes of entertainment
and your desperation hanging from your pockets.
I could see it clearly,
how awkward.

A confession

I used to swear I'd never
sit on the same side of the restaurant booth as you
or anyone for that matter.
I've always equated it
to shining a spotlight
a bright bulb,
on the couple
who can't be apart from each other
long enough to finish a meal.

But on a Sunday night in a deli
where the only lovers are over the age of sixty-seven,
I decide I can make an exception.
As you eat matzoh ball soup for the first time
I have a closer hand
to both yours and the food
I know you won't finish.

With this view,
we make a drive-in out of the diner.
The rest of the patrons, a scene
for us to watch in unison.
Smiling,
enjoying the lack of
space between our beings.

This closeness,
is a privilege I used to shake my head at,
mock in disgust
before I knew how it was
to be this content with someone.
It's an easy thing to dismiss a sort of happiness
before you understand it.
There is certainly a kind of magic
that comes with a lack of distance.

Beyond existing

Today is not the first day of my life.
I am appreciating what it means to have lived.

I am learning how to flip a record on its back.
Looking at our hands, halves curling into a whole.
Writing as a waterfall
all flowing, no pause
all heart.
Smiling through cracked lips in the center of Detroit,
warmth conquering winter.

I think in these moments
I really am alive,
aren't I?
Life is more than just a coincidence,
isn't it?

I am meant for more than stillness,
destined to be all the opposite of the quiet
I have begged to be.
I am refusing to take silence as a second name.

I am alive in the grit of teeth
in the soft space of the inner elbow
in the finger prints of my love.

This isn't the first day of my life
but what if I were to live it as so?
as if I were just now grasping
what it means to be alive...

beyond just existing.

ACKNOWLEDGEMENTS

Thank you to my parents, who support me, always, without question. To Ari, for being the hand that led me to poetry (and ultimately to this collection). To the poets I admire who have constantly supported, encouraged, and inspired me. To Kat, for her undaunted passion, mentorship, and hard work. To Say Word LA for being the organization that gave me a second home. To Julia, my illustrator, for her amazing work as well as her courage (and many talents). To my professors, both Glaser and Osborn, for allowing me to explore the heart within academia. To anyone who has ever found comfort in words I have written. To anyone who struggled to make it to today, but still did.

@danielleshorr
Danielleshorr.com

Made in the USA
San Bernardino, CA
13 December 2016